MY PAIN, MY BODY, MY LIFE

Carmine Tulino

AuthorHouse™
1663 Liberty Drive
Bloomington, IN 47403
www.authorhouse.com
Phone: 1 (800) 839-8640

Published by AuthorHouse 10/05/2018

ISBN: 978-1-5462-5514-7 (sc)
ISBN: 978-1-5462-5513-0 (e)

Library of Congress Control Number: 2018907724

Print information available on the last page.

This book is printed on acid-free paper.

authorHOUSE®

MY PAIN,
MY BODY,
MY LIFE

CHAPTER 1

JUNE 22, 2009

It's my birthday. I'm fifty-three. Looking back at all the times I've been cut open and operated on, I recall times I felt like one of those animals used to teach dissection in science class.

I'll never forget the second time I had to get my spine fused; that operation took twenty-two hours. A funny part happened when I was being prepped for the surgery. A nurse had to insert a catheter into a private part of my body. I was not totally under anesthesia, and when the nurse started to go about inserting the tube, I became fully erect. That's something I don't remember. But I was told I had also grabbed her ass. That became the talk of the hospital. For the twenty-two hours the doctors had their hands in me, they couldn't stop laughing.

When I came to in the recovery room, everyone from the doctors' staff came over to see how I was doing. Everyone joked when the doctors came by. The first thing out of one doctor's mouth was, "God has blessed you." He laughed. I couldn't figure out what was so funny. But after his third visit, he finally told me what had happened.

I still have the cast that was used on my foot when I was born. It's so small that I can't fit even two fingers in it.

I grew up in Bensonhurst with five siblings in a house with a big backyard. My father bought a swing set. Instead of swinging back and forth, I swung side to side. A bolt that was sticking out cut a hole in my hip. That was my first tattoo. I ended up with so many scars that I decided to just call them tattoos.

One time when I was nine, I ju-mped up on the kitchen counter next to the sink to get the box of Captain Crunch on the top shelf. The door was open a little, just enough to put a hole in the top of my head. Three more stitches. Boy, after fifty-three years, my head looks like a golf course.

I didn't stop there. As I got older, I just got more daring like riding my bike down a hill in the park just to show off. One time, I thought I'd just make it between the trees and stop before the fence, but two more stitches in the left elbow told me I was wrong.

Then I was introduced to minibikes, and I can't forget about the martial art practice of learning how to deal with pain. I was starting to think that I could stop a train and nothing could hurt me.

It was on a perfect summer day when everyone had something to do and somewhere to go. Even my parents had gone away that weekend. Dennis and I had to work until 5:30 that day, and all our friends had gone to the Hamptons. My father had left his car, a new Cutlass Supreme, in the driveway. We needed a car, and I just happened to have a spare key. We took off for the Hamptons for some dining and dancing on the beach and a lot of girls. With money in our pockets, we were two wild and crazy guys.

We needed to rest after working all day because we were planning on partying all night. I also had to get my father's car back by early Monday afternoon. Dennis took a nap on the way up, so it was my turn to rest on the way home. Dennis also decided to take a nap while he was driving. The car wrapped around a tree at sixty miles per hour.

I woke up in a hospital with tubes running down a pole and into my arm, and my face felt funny. My front teeth were missing. They had come out through my upper lip.

We had both been out for about twelve hours. My father's car was totaled. It was a miracle we hadn't been killed. I felt really bad about the car because my dad loved it.

Sorry, Pop!

CHAPTER 2

MOTORCYCLES

Because I worked in a motorcycle shop, I always had a new Kawasaki. When I rode down the block on one wheel at high speeds, people watched with their mouths open thinking they were seeing Evel Knievel.

Right after the Fourth of July, I sold a KZ900 to my friend Charlie. The bike looked great parked next to his XJ-12 Jaguar convertible. Right before Labor Day, he brought the bike in for service. I talked him into buying a set of headers for the bike and changing the jets in the carburetors. We made that bike fly!

I took it out for a test run. Boy, it was just like the bike had a jet engine. When I cracked the throttle, my eyes sunk into the back of my skull.

I knew that right before you went over an old bridge on Stillwell Avenue in Coney Island to the beach, there was never any traffic. And when I turned onto Stillwell, no one was in sight—just the way I wanted. Perfect.

I accelerated. The front wheel came up. I felt I went from zero to sixty in three seconds—and I was still just in second gear. I threw it into third. The bike was screaming as I passed ninety miles per hour.

Life stops when you're doing a hundred miles per hour. A second seems like forever. You're in the third dimension when everything around you is at a standstill. I heard what people were thinking without hearing them. I spoke to people who had been dead for years in all that silence. I could have been in a rainstorm or a snowstorm and not have felt the rain or the cold. The same went for pain.

Everything was at a standstill, but everything was moving. There must have been hundreds of people talking, but I couldn't hear what they were saying. There was no time. People came around and went off, but there were no cars, buses, trains, or planes. You can go so far into the third dimension and never see the same thing twice. You just kept on going and going, but you never come back.

Someone called me, and that time, it was different. The voice prompted me to turn around. My grandmother told me to go home because it was getting late.

Then my eyes opened. It felt I had just closed them, but later, I learned that I had been in a coma for two and a half months. It still felt the same, but I couldn't move or talk. All I saw were lights and strange people. All I could hear was my grandma saying, "Come home."

I'd been a fly that had met a flyswatter when I was doing ninety down Stillwell Avenue. An oil truck had made a U-turn right in front of me. I hit the truck so hard that I broke the driver's leg.

I was out of the coma, but things were very different. I couldn't remember what had happened to me. My head was shaved. I couldn't talk or walk. My left arm felt funny. The doctors had put an internal cast in my arm. They screwed a plate against the bone, which was in pieces, hoping it would fuse. I had broken my spine. I had cut my throat so badly that they had to drill six holes in my head to relieve the pressure. Everyone kept saying it was a miracle that I had survived.

I had to learn how to walk and talk. It was hard, but I didn't stop trying. It was really hard to move because my spine was broken. I had a brace wrapped around my midsection.

Three and a half weeks later, I was out of the hospital. The first thing I did was visit my grandma. She was praying and holding her rosary. She said, "I knew you'd be home soon! I was waiting for you!" A short time after that, she passed away. She will always be with me and looking out for me. She is my god.

Two months later, I got right back on a motorcycle. Motorcycles aren't dangerous, but those who ride them can be.

Left Forearm   First cast after two days

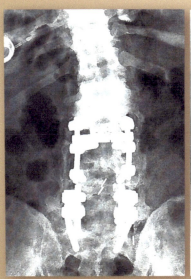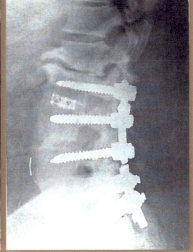

My Spine

CHAPTER 3

MY HORSEBACK RIDING ADVENTURE

Even a year or so after my motorcycle accident, my body hadn't fully recovered. My spine was still broken, but I didn't trust anyone to cut me open and mess with my spine.

It was fall. I can't say I had bad luck that fall because I'm still here to write about it.

My friend Larry Mangano had taken me and some other friends to Wildwood, New Jersey, for a fishing weekend. We had a great time and caught a lot of big fish. I enjoyed driving the boat.

Back onshore, they started to clean the fish and build a campfire. It was getting late, and we were hungry. I had never had barbecued fish like that before. It tasted really good. We even had some of my father's homemade wine, which made it even better.

The next day, we decided to go horseback riding. I didn't care too much for horseback riding especially because my back was still broken, but they all assured me they'd go slowly, which they did.

We started out early that morning; we had packed lunches in our saddles. We walked our horses to the beach and rode along the water. We tied the horses to a tree, took a nap, threw a

Frisbee around, and drank some more wine. We were having a great day. It was a good thing that the others were all real cowboys. I'd gone to a rodeo and watched them jump off horses onto bulls and wrestle them to the ground. That made me feel a little safe. I rode my horse bareback that day because they told me it would make the horse a little calmer.

The sun was starting to go down when we neared the stable. Larry started to gallop, and all the horses did too. The path was pretty wide at one point, but a tree stood in the middle; the path went around the tree on both sides. Wouldn't you know it—as I was passing the tree on the right, my horse must have gotten scared by something that made him jump over to the left side of the tree while I was passing it. That move left me hanging off the right side of my horse.

I remember waking up in the hospital. It turned out that when I was hanging off the right side of the horse, the tree used my head for batting practice. I had been out for two hours. That was the last time I was on a horse .Everyone said I had nine lives.

CHAPTER 4

BRACE YOURSELF

About six months after my motorcycle accident, a funny thing happened every time I bumped my elbow into anything—it would blow up into a ball. At first, I thought it had something to do with the plate that was bolted to my forearm bone to hold its six pieces together.

After going to the hospital and getting an x-ray, the doctors found a piece of glass that had traveled through my body. It had entered through my neck that had been cut open when my head went through the truck door and broke the driver's leg. It had traveled from my neck to my elbow. While the doctors were taking the glass out, I had asked them to take the plate out also. The bone was healed, and the plate was not needed. My body was hurting, especially my back. My spine was still broken, so I had to wear a brace for support.

While I was in the hospital, they showed me a way to strengthen my stomach muscles that gave me the same support as the back brace. At times when I wasn't wearing my brace and was so relaxed, without thinking, I'd pick up something or take a fast turn and my nerves stuck between my broken spine and my legs would just give out and I'd fall. It's scary when you can't move your legs. When that would happen, I'd stay in bed and take pills to relax the muscles.

It was like that for five years until I met Dr. Casden, the leading spinal surgeon in New York. After looking at my spine, he suggested I get a bone fusion. He said that fusing three vertebrae had never been done before and that the operation would take twenty-two hours. They'd have to cut two pieces of bone from my hip to be screwed into my spine; that's what bone fusion is. Eventually, the bones would bond.

The operation was a success. I felt like a new man. I even started to lift weights—pump iron. Very carefully, I started to train in the gym every day. I even took the exam to become a bus driver.

A year later, I received a letter telling me I had been accepted and was to start training. I started to work for the transit system on February 2, 2000. My depot was in Staten Island, and one of my runs was an express from Staten Island to Manhattan. I was on top of the world. I took everyone to work in the morning and picked them up at night; I had two runs in the morning and three at night. The routes would change every six months, but I still got to know all the passengers because I saw them every day.

The best time was in the summer. I let some of the girls who wore short skirts ride for free. Some of them had legs that could stop a herd of wild animals. I know. I was one of those wild animals.

I got close to Maryann. She was always the first person on line at the first stop, so she always sat in the first-row seat to my right. We became good friends. She was such a friendly person, and she had the prettiest legs on Staten Island.

One day, everything started off the same; I picked up all my morning regulars and was on my way to the city through the Battery Tunnel. My first stop was the World Trade Center. Maryann was always the first one off the bus. That day, she touched the back of my head when she said goodbye. That touch sent chills down my back. It was the way her fingers went through my hair and that look in her eyes. I felt as if I were driving or should I say flying a magic carpet.

As I pulled away, it seemed like déjà vu. People started pointing up. Everyone was in the street. I stopped the bus. Everyone on the bus was getting excited and saying a plane had crashed into the World Trade Center. My heart stopped. All I thought about was Maryann. I saw flames shooting out of the top of the building. Before I knew it, another plane hit the other tower. I wanted to go back. Everyone was in shock. I saw people just falling out of the building. I was instructed to go through the Lincoln Tunnel and get the bus back to the depot. I was thinking about Maryann when I started to drive away. I looked in my rearview mirror, and all I could see was a big black wall of smoke.

I was instructed not to drop off the rest of passengers; I was to bring the bus in. Some passengers stayed on the bus. Most of them were crying; the rest of us were scared. We heard sirens everywhere—fire trucks and ambulances coming from every direction.

When I got back to Staten Island and saw everything on TV, life stopped again. Nobody was talking. Everyone was trying to get in contact with friends or spouses who worked in the area, but all the phones weren't working. Luckily for me, I got in touch with my wife and learned she was all right.

The next day, soldiers were stopping all traffic going into and out of Manhattan. The city buses and first responders were the only ones going through the Battery Tunnel. The walls of the tunnel was covered with … I don't know what it was, but it was gray, and I saw paper everywhere. People on the bus were going back to see what was left; we were instructed not to let anyone bring packages onto the bus without going through them.

It was scary coming out of the Battery Tunnel and looking around. The scene was right out of an old war movie. Nothing was the same after that. Smoke was still coming out of the rubble that had once been the World Trade Center. No one was allowed into that area. City buses were allowed to drive around the block instead of through it. Everyone on the bus had his or her face against the windows. Some were crying. I drove very slowly and saw firefighters and police working together trying to find anybody who was still alive.

I stopped the bus and started to cry thinking about Maryann. I realized she had had enough time to get up to her job, which had been in the area of impact. I had to drive through that every day; I lost all interest and joy in driving the bus. All the broken bones I had were nothing like the pain of a broken heart.

Three months later, I was transferred to the garage to work on bus maintenance. I couldn't forget the horror of 9/11 and the friend I'd lost that day. I started to change in every way—my looks and the way I took care of myself. I got sloppy with my habits—you know, drinking a little, getting a little fat. One time, I twisted my ankle climbing into a bus but ignored it until about six months later, when I finally went in for surgery. My ankle was hurting and was always swollen.

CHAPTER 5

VIRGINIA BEACH

After the surgery, I was in a cast for three months. I was going crazy doing nothing. One day, I went for a ride to Virginia Beach to see some friends I had not seen for a long time. I hopped around Virginia with one leg in a cast until I stopped, rested a bit, and looked at all that was around me. I saw little buses that looked like trolley cars taking people back and forth along the beach. Across the road, I saw a little house with a For Sale sign in the front yard. I fell in love with the place. I ended up putting $500 down on my credit card, and my mortgage was only $749 a month. I couldn't have asked for anything better than that. New York City Transit was paying my mortgage, and I was living like a king. To me, being a beach bum was even better than being a king. I became friends with everyone.

I even bought stock in the town bank; when I walked into the bank, it was not "Can I help you?" or "Next in line"; it was, "Hi, Mr. Tulino. Can I help you?"

I even transferred my driver's license and registered my car in Virginia. I'd sit on a bench by the beach and watch fighter jets taking off from and landing on the base; they were so close that I could wave to the pilots. They'd fly slowly and only about 200 feet off the ground and then suddenly like a rocket ship, they'd take off up into the sky with engines roaring and never stop going; they would disappear like the space shuttles would.

It wasn't long before I met the locals, and they were all so friendly. I was living in a fantasy land. I was still wearing the cast on my foot, and all my neighbors would stop by to see if there was anything they could do for me. Doretta, one neighbor, was a great cook. She'd always invite me over for dinner and a martini.

I find it hard to describe how grateful I was to have found this place. Every day was wonderful, a carbon copy of the previous day—not to hot and not to cold. I knew I'd have to go back to New York, but I wanted to find a way to move to Virginia Beach.

During the holiday season, I had a new car and went for a ride to see family in New Jersey. I left my mother's house on my way to Staten Island to visit my kids, and I stopped for a red light on Route 9. I remember that just like that, I started to see all these people. The funny thing was that I saw everybody before I spotted a girl crying but with no tears. It was crazy hearing that sound as if it were coming from inside a barrel. If you put a lid on the barrel, the sound would stop, but I still saw people understanding each other just like déjà vu. It was so familiar not being scared; there was nothing to be scared of because I couldn't feel anything.

One thing that really stood out was an old man facing in the opposite direction pointing back. When I turn around, I saw a blinding light. I saw people's mouths moving. Some were pulling me and asking me if I could move, but I couldn't respond because I had a mask over my mouth to help me breathe. I hear the familiar sound of a siren; I was being taken to the hospital.

It turned out that while I had been waiting for that red light to turn green, a truck rear-ended me and ripped my car open. The driver didn't even put on his brakes. It's a good thing he turned at the last minute so he didn't drive directly into my car, but nevertheless, he ripped open my car as if it were a can of tuna. The impact was hard enough to put me back in that world I had been so happy to have come back from.

I was in the hospital again going through those familiar tests. I had no car; I was in pain, but I was surprised to be living. I was far from my new home that I wished I had never left.

Time went by slowly. The only good thing I had going for me was that my family was all around me. After I got out of the hospital, they drove me to all kinds of specialists, but none of them could figure out why I felt pain in my back. I felt just like I did before I had the first bone fusion on my spine. I saw the doctor I had so much confidence in—Dr. Casden—after the doctors in New Jersey and therapists couldn't help me. Dr. Casden x-rayed me and discovered why I was in pain. He showed me on the x-ray where my problem was and why. He said that to eliminate the pain, my fused vertebrae would have to be disassembled and some new ones put in. He said he wouldn't have to take bone out of my hip; there was a new material they could use, but the operation would take twelve hours. That was better than the twenty-two hours my last spinal surgery had taken though.

"Thanks, Doc," I said. I had so much confidence in Dr. Casden that people thought I was losing it after I told them I was excited about going under the knife again. Dr. Casden came through, however. I was once again recovering from another major and successful surgery.

But time wasn't waiting for me to catch up, and I was finding it harder to keep up. I was slowing down. I wasn't as mobile as before. I found it harder to walk, and the less I walked, the fatter I got of course. I wanted to lose weight, so I figured I'd look at the medical field for help. I mean, I'd been under the knife so many times that an operation for a lap band would be like going for a manicure. But undergoing any operation big or small requires the same procedures—tests and being poked by needles to draw blood among them. The only thing different was the shorter hospital stay.

　　After the operation, I expected my excess weight would just melt away. At first, it did, but as I got more comfortable with my eating habits, the weight just stopped coming off. I found that I still had to exercise and watch what I ate.

CHAPTER 6

GROWING UP IN BROOKLYN

My short-term memory is bad, but I can remember things that happened when I was three years old and growing up in Brooklyn. I remember walking to the Williamsburg Bank with my mother. That was when my two older sisters were in school. I wasn't old enough for school, but I remember walking down Fourth Avenue and Atlantic to this giant building with a big clock on top you could see from far away. Inside, I was amazed at how high the ceiling was.

The Brooklyn Dodgers had their last game in Ebbets Field on Atlantic Avenue. They moved in 1956, the year I was born. Whenever anyone in our house was sick, someone would go across the street to the drug store and see Sam. On his way home from work, my father would stop at Sam's to pick up anything needed whenever someone wasn't feeling good at home. My grandfather owned the building we lived in and the one around the corner, where my uncle, aunt, and cousin lived on the top floor and my grandmother and grandfather lived on the ground floor.

My grandfather would give my cousin and me a quarter each, and we felt rich with those quarters. We'd go to a candy store next door from my cousin's apartment building and come out with bags of candy along with a pack of baseball cards. We'd sit all afternoon on the sidewalk flipping cards and eating candy.

One day, my cousin and I tried to fix a flat tire on my bike on the sidewalk in front of his house, which was so much wider than the sidewalk around the corner where I lived.

Things were great when I started kindergarten. I'd pass a place called Miss Smith's; I could smell the pies they made from a long way off. The owner would give away pieces of pies that had broken broke or hadn't come out of the oven good enough to sell. Those day are gone.

Things around the neighborhood were starting to change; the nights started to get rough. I remember sitting by the window with my mother waiting for my father to come home from work. My father was a plumber, he used to do side jobs at night, and he always worked on Sunday.

We'd take a ride to my other grandfather's house; it was an exciting ride. I'd lift up a mat and look through a hole in the floor between the front seat and the back seat; I'd watch the road go by.

My grandfather had such a big house; he had a basketball court in the back, a huge garden on the side, and a tremendous front yard. My father always took different routes home from my grandfather's house. I didn't know why he did that then, but I do now. My parents were house shopping because my father really wanted to move away from downtown Brooklyn. It was getting dangerous especially at night. There was a fight almost every night, and people were doing drugs and drinking.

One night, I heard sirens and people yelling—the cops were everywhere looking for someone. My mother kept telling me to get away from the window. The next day, my mother was crying. I found out someone had shot and killed Sam at the drugstore for drugs.

The area got really bad; my mother was always yelling at me not to leave the front of the house. One day, two boys who lived in the building next door were playing with an old refrigerator box; that looked like fun. They were laughing and kept calling me. The box was at the bottom of the steps; when I got close enough to see what they were laughing about, they pulled me in and sexually assaulted me. One kid had his pants open, and the other pushed my head down towards his crotch. I'd never been so scared. No matter how much I tried to get away or even scream, they outnumbered and overpowered me.

I finally got away and ran upstairs crying. My aunt was there helping my mother, who was pregnant and having contractions. My aunt yelled at me and told me to stay away from those boys. I never told anyone till now; this is the first time I ever said anything about it. I was only four, about to turn five, and the neighborhood was no longer safe especially at night.

On September 1, 1960, my mother gave birth to my brother and sister, twins Vincent and Nancy. Everyone was so happy. I met relatives I never knew we had. But our apartment was getting tight. One Saturday, we drove out to what I thought was the country but it was only Bensonhurst. My father parked in front of a real big house and told my sister and me that this was our new home. The twins were too small, so they stayed with my grandparents.

Our new house was big; a narrow staircase I though had been made especially for me led from the second floor to the attic. The backyard was so big, and the house had a really big basement. The train to Coney Island was only two blocks from our house; we were only a couple of stops from 86th Street and Bay Parkway. Williamsburg Bank was on 86th Street and 23rd Avenue. It wasn't that big, but it too had a high ceiling. St. Mary's, my new school, was on 85th Street and 23rd Avenue. Back then, I was always moving around and not particularly quiet at school. The nuns who taught us carried pointers to point things out on the blackboard and to whack our hands if we weren't paying attention or interrupting them. That was just a warning. If someone misbehaved again, he or she would get smacked on the back of the thigh. That would leave a big red mark. When my mother saw a red mark on me, she went to school and let them know she didn't like her son being hit like that.

I caught a lot of flak at home for not being an A student. The next school year, I started at PS 101, a public school. After the first week, my mother allowed me to walk the four blocks to school with Steve, a neighbor who was older, and Joe, who was Steve's cousin who lived across the street. My mother felt more relaxed that I wasn't alone.

As I got older, my friends and I became more daring and adventurous by riding our bikes farther from home. A path we called the bicycle path went past Nelly Bly Amusement Park along the water all the way downtown to the Staten Island Ferry dock. I stood out among my friends for having no fear going fast on a bike. And I would always somehow get the money to ride go-karts on the track. I'd push the pedal way down to go as fast as I could. If anyone got in front of me, I'd run him off the road.

My father started taking me with him on his side jobs; I'd carry tools to and from the car. Before you knew it, I was good at being his helper. I could fit under sinks and could maneuver in other tight spots, and my father became confident I'd do a good job.

But one time, I screwed up. We had just finished a big job, and I was putting the chrome fixtures back on a tub when I dropped a screw down the drain. Boy, my father got so mad because he had to take the whole thing apart to get that screw. He cursed in Italian the whole time, and we didn't get home till midnight. I cry now thinking of all the things I put that man through. But I'd make a lot of money selling the old brass, lead, and copper we'd get from all the remodeling we did.

CHAPTER 7

FERTILIZER

After my father retired, he started gardening, and he loved it. Everything he grew tasted so good; I guess it was the way he did it. One day, he had asked me to go with him to buy some fertilizer. I said we could take my car, which was a rental I had to get back later that day. I told him that way, his car would stay clean and I'd have less work.

Don't forget that fertilizer is horse manure. The horse stable was off the Belt Parkway down by Rockaway Beach. All the way there, my father kept asking me if I had brought the heavy garbage bags to put the manure in. We got to the horse stable and gave the stableman $5. He said, "Help yourself" and pointed to a pile of horseshit twenty feet high and thirty feet wide. What a smell! And we hadn't brought masks.

My father kept asking about the bags, and I kept saying he shouldn't worry about it. He thought they were in the trunk. I didn't want to stay around that pile of shit much longer, so I backed the car up to the pile of manure, opened the trunk, and started to shovel the shit into the trunk. My father started to yell and curse in Italian, and the more he cursed, the faster I shoveled. I packed that trunk with so much shit that the trunk lid had to be slammed. Boy, that trunk was really full of shit.

My father and I laughed so hard all the way home; we didn't know if we were crying due to the scent of the shit or the thought of what they would say when I brought back the rental. But my father's garden was well fertilized. When I took the car back, I told the people in the office that the car really stunk and quickly left the office.

After that, whenever I'd say, "That stinks!" at Sunday dinner when the whole family was there, I would look at my father and we'd laugh hard; no one knew why. That's a part of life a person never forgets.

MINIBIKES

Down by the bay, they had filled in the inlet and had built a shopping center with a Korvettes, a big department store. The place was closed on Sundays, so everyone would race their go-karts and minibikes around the parking lot. I bought my first minibike for $30. It was a real piece of junk, but I'd ride it around the lot. I would fall frequently because the chain would get jammed and the wheel would lock up.

Every Sunday when I got home, my mother would see my cuts and bruises and tell me, "You come home all the time with another injury and cuts. You're covered in bruises. Get rid of that stupid thing before you kill yourself!"

So I started to work out, and I found a karate school. I was impressed by the instructor, who endured the pain of smashing cinder blocks on his stomach and punching through boards. I thought karate was just the thing for me. I walked four miles to the school and four miles home. I started to train every day. One day, I saw a minibike in the window of a bike shop on Avenue U and East 5th Street. It was like super minibike with a 50 cc, five-speed, two-cycle engine. I'd go in and sit on it for a long time when there were no customers there.

I got to know the owner, and he let me work building cycle wheels. I would lace the hub with spokes and build racing wheels. I got very good at it; I built fifty wheels in just one Saturday. I was also good at fixing bikes in the repair shop there. The bike shop was only six blocks from the karate school, so I'd go there after work.

My body was getting tougher and stronger, and I made enough to buy that Bonanza minibike. People were amazed to see my minibike go faster than all those go-karts on Sundays at the Korvettes' parking lot. I always wanted to go faster.

I learned about the sport of motocross racing, and soon, that 50 cc minibike became a 250 cc motocross racing bike. I would have to have that bike taken to and from wherever there was a race. Times were good; the bike store became a Kawasaki dealership.

CHAPTER 9

ANKLE PROBLEMS AND A CADDY

Time doesn't stop. It's been a year maybe longer since I read this, and I have to say my writing has matured, or maybe I'm just getting older. Anyway, in the past year, I got hurt again in the bus yard going into the office. Pieces of wood were used as steps to climb up out of the yard through an electric security gate that would lock at 6:00 p.m. One time as I was going through, the wooden step gave way and came out from under me. The gate had square metal poles, and my ankle ended up between my body and the pole. The edge of the pole had scraped a layer of bone off my outer left ankle, so I had to wear an ankle brace. And my lap band had to come out because I decided to get a sleeve in its place—that's where they cut out half of your stomach.

Time really won't stop for you or anyone else. Time is life, and when you look back in time, you can look back at your life, and every time you look back, you'll always find something.

I live in New Jersey now, and there's still a little bit country here. I see a lot of animals. I found a buffalo farm; they are really beautiful animals. Some farms host rodeos, so rodeos bring back memories. I wrote about my friend Larry who rode horses. I used to go and watch him at rodeos. He competed in bull-dogging—jumping off a horse, tackling a cow, and tying its legs just to see who could do it in the least amount of time.

When I was fifteen, I went along with Larry to a rodeo because he was always bragging about how good he was. And he was pretty good, but he couldn't ride wild bulls too good.

One time after a rodeo, all the cowboys went to a saloon and were having a good time bullshitting about the rodeo. I was only a sixteen-year-old Brooklyn boy with about fifteen cowboys in this little saloon in the middle of nowhere that had a dance floor. All the locals would hang out there. Well, I made my way over to the dance floor and saw this cute little blonde, and we started to rock on the dance floor. Beer was flowing to all the cowboys, and I asked Larry for the car key because I was too young to drink in a bar. I wanted to sit in the car with the girl I had met. She and I decided to go down the block a little where there were fewer people than there were in the parking lot.

Larry's Caddy had impressed the girl especially after I told her it was mine. After all my sweet talking, I had her just where I wanted her. Just as we started to get into steaming up the windows, a knock on the car window surprised us. A cop car had come out of nowhere, and a police officer was standing outside our car with a night stick. He asked all kinds of questions, and he wanted to see a license and registration, but I didn't even have a wallet.

He got us both out of the car. That was back in the seventies when the country was the country and a New York boy in a Caddy stood out especially when the Caddy was blocking part of the driveway where the officer parked his squad car. The police station was just across the street, and it looked like the one in Mayberry in the *Andy Griffith Show*.

I'd forgotten I was in a little town. After the fact came out that I was only sixteen, the officer asked how the car had gotten to where it was. I told him she had driven it because she was old enough to drive and had a license.

He made her pull the car up to the corner where all the cowboys were still partying. The officer went in to see if our story made any sense. Don't forget I was not only too young to drive but also too young to be in a bar drinking.

The officer along with all the rodeo cowboys came out of the bar. The cowboys were all yahooing, patting me on the shoulder, and putting their cowboy hats on me, making me feel good for having scored with an older woman.

CHAPTER 10

I REMEMBER LOUIE

When you get old, you can just close your eyes and look back in time and remember the people who made your life memorable. For me, one such person is Louie.

Whenever we went anywhere, we would always have to wait for Louie because it would take him so long to fix his hair. He would sing like Elvis Presley as he looked in the mirror. He didn't have a job at the time I was living in an apartment, the attic of my parents' house. I decided to renovate it by knocking down the wall that was between the kitchen and dining room. Louie helped me. He was great at destroying things.

Once we got the wall down, we had a big mess to lug three flights down. Even after three trips, we still had a lot of stuff to bring down. We decided to take out a window at the top of the stairway on the side of the house and throw everything out the hole. Great idea, but it made a big mess of my father's bocce ball court.

We always took breaks to smoke cigarettes. After one break, we turned to this 250-pound cast iron radiator. We looked at it then at each other and got the same idea to throw it out the window instead of carrying it down all those steps. The radiator was long. We got one end up and resting on the windowsill. We had started to lift the other end up to slide it out when I heard someone calling my name. We stopped trying to shove the radiator out the window.

My mother was right down below house yelling, "Carmine? What are you doing?" Holy shit! If we'd let that thing go out that window, it would have not only hit my mother but also planted her in the ground. But when the shock was over, we had something to laugh about for a long time.

Another time, Louie and I were hooking up my TV antenna. I set up a folding ladder on the fire escape so I could climb on the roof. I got on the roof, but I couldn't get down because the edge of the roof overlapped the ladder, so I couldn't see it from up on the roof. Louie was too busy drawing pictures in the closet. I must have been stuck on that roof for at least an hour before Louie heard me. But my apartment really came out looking good.

When he was young, Louie liked to burn things with magnifying glasses or matches, and he never lost his fascination with fire.

When we were older, we started going to clubs on Saturday nights in cars someone would lend us. Vito, who later in life became my brother-in-law, worked in a body shop. He had just finished working on a Caddy El Dorado convertible—a beautiful car.

One perfect summer night on our way home from the Penthouse Club bombed out of our heads, a drunken Vito went too fast around a turn and sideswiped a car. We were all drunk, so we kept on going until we realized what we'd done.

We pulled over to look at the damage to the Caddy. On Vito's first night with the Caddy, he'd smashed the side quarter panel. Four of us looked at the damage and just laughed. Louie told Vito we should just burn the car because we'd left the scene of the accident.

The car was a showpiece—green with white interior. Vito said he'd tell his father that someone had stolen it; he was sure the insurance company would pay for a new one. After a while with all the laughing, Louie finally got Vito to ease up, and there was Louie with his lighter. Before you knew it, the car was in flames. We were all standing there looking at it burn. Out of nowhere, Louie started to laugh. We asked him what he was laughing about, and he said, "So how are we going to get home?" He started yelling at Vito for burning his car. Another night out I'll never forget.

About a year after Louie and I had renovated my apartment, he passed away. He was a great friend, and I always think about him and will never forget him.

CHAPTER 11

SOMETHING BOTTLED UP

My life was screwed up. I thought about all the things I had done and all the thing I should have done. I thought about all the things that had happened to me. I guess I was coming out of the dark.

After all the accidents I had, and after all the times I told people, "I don't care," I realized I'd bottled up something inside and couldn't find a way to let it out. After all these years, I find it easy to write about it. After all, this book is about me, and today, many people are opening up about things in their pasts they had kept hidden.

I mentioned earlier about how I had been sexually abused by those older kids when I was only four. Now, I see what's going on. Today, people are fortunately taking child sexual abuse more seriously. I wished my experience of being sexually abused had stopped there, but it did not.

When I was about ten, there was a man who lived in the neighborhood with a wood shop in his basement; he made things for my family. He was friendly with everyone. One day, he took my cousin and me to his workshop where he showed us some dirty movies, which we laughed at.

Another day, I went to see my grandmother and grandfather, who lived in the same house as my cousin. He called me over and started to talk about that movie. He touched me and wanted me to come down to his basement to look at what he said was a different movie.

The look in his eyes was creepy, and the way he touched me was more like a scary pull or a push with his hand on my butt. I was only ten, but these things stay in your mind forever. I wish that it would have stopped, and it did for a while.

Two maybe three years went by, and we got a little bit more independent and curious. We'd ride our bikes farther from home and explore more of the neighborhood. One day, we rode by an alley on Bath Avenue and decided to explore it. We spotted a big black door with no lock, so we opened it. We saw that it was the exit to the Deluxe Movie Theater, which showed porn. We found we could get in any time we wanted to, and we did.

Time went on. My mother was a real good person. She took care of babies who had been abandoned and left at the Guardian Angel Home. My mother watched children there, and she became a foster mother for some until they were placed in homes. She had taken care of many babies.

One day, my mother yelled for help. I went into the room before my father did, and I saw that the baby my mother was caring for was not moving; his skin was a different color. The baby had died in his sleep. That was the first time I really got scared. I started to scream. I ran into my father's arms.

My mother stopped taking care of little kids for a while. About six months later, my mother took care of a sixteen-year-old girl. She was a wild one, too much for my mother to handle.

One day, she showed my cousin and me her tits. She was really free with herself. We were swimming in the backyard pool when she got frisky and grabbed my nuts. We went to my father's wine cellar, and I got my first blow job before I was thirteen. My mother knew something was happening; I call it mother's intuition. The girl was gone by the next week.

When I got into junior high, I was a real ladies' man, a real smooth talker. And that movie house was still there; no one had fixed that door. I was always asking girls out and telling them I had a pass to the movies.

One girl who liked me came with me to the movies, but she was shocked at what was playing. We didn't stay at the movie long, but later back in my basement as we were watching TV, she nearly raped me. I didn't mind. We didn't go all the way because my family was right upstairs, we were still underage, and it was still light outside. But it seemed we kissed for hours.

I realize now how much porn can affect people's minds especially those who start to watch porn at age fourteen. Forty-five years later, I enjoy watching porn. It's a way to get the fire going when you're watching it with someone who can share the passion and enjoy great sex.

CHAPTER 12

MORE ANKLE SURGERY AND LOST SHOES TOO

The spring of 2015 was déjà vu all over again. I couldn't walk again; I felt paralyzed. Thank God it wasn't as bad as before; there was a time when I couldn't walk because of what was supposed to be a simple reconstructive ankle operation.

The operation went perfectly, but the recovery not so well. After one week, the doctor took off the Ace bandage that was holding a cardboard boot that would soon become a cast. The doctor pushed in the side of the cardboard to check the stitches and make sure everything was all right. Everything was. A nurse came in and asked me what color I would like for my cast, and I picked black. He started to wrap black gauze around the cardboard boot that would harden into a cast. The only problem was that he forgot to straighten out the cardboard; when the cast got hard, that made the cardboard dig into my ankle right over the stitches. The more the cardboard got tighter and cut into the ankle, the more it swelled up.

After a week, I was experiencing an unbelievable and indescribable amount of pain. The cardboard had cut in so far that blood was dripping out from the hole in the cast for my toes. When the doctor took the cast off, my foot was covered with blood. And it got infected twice.

He started me on therapy, but that just made the pain worse. Even the inside of my ankle swelled up and hurt incredibly. With a bad ankle, I found walking was uncomfortable, and I felt unstable. One day when I was vacuuming, I tripped over the cord and landed on my knees. The next day, my knee was bad. That with my bad ankle made me feel crippled again. I had the empty feeling I'd had when I was paralyzed after all this started.

To make matters worse, I got some bad news—my old friend Charlie Denoto died. I had been trying to get in touch with him for almost a year after I had learned his wife had passed away. I found out in a weird way that he died; my cousin told me after he heard it from a friend. I had stayed in touch with his sister, who still lived in Brooklyn, where we had all grown up. We used to go fishing by the bay, which was two blocks from home.

I wrote about racing go-karts and minibikes in the Korvettes parking lot near there. One time, Charlie bought a minibike from a Gypsy for $10 and sold it to me for $15. It was a piece of shit, but I got hooked on riding it. Around that time, I started to work at that bike shop and saved up enough to buy that 50 cc Bonanza four-speed minibike. There was no turning back; I was hooked on racing bikes.

Charlie was a real good looking guy. When we went to clubs, he attracted all the girls, and I reeled them in and took them home. One night, I met a good-looking woman who was older than me. We were out in Charlie's car that night, so he dropped us off at her house. She was a real wild woman, and wouldn't you know it? We heard a noise downstairs. She said, "Holy shit! My husband's home!" Just like you would see on TV, I grabbed my clothes and jumped out the window, but I had forgotten my shoes, so I was barefoot.

Later that night, I met Charlie and told him about my adventure; we laughed because I had no shoes. We got back in his car looking to party some more. I still don't know why Charlie went back to that woman's house to get my shoes; I guess that was Charlie's way of being fearless. I think he was feeling his oats. After two shots of Johnnie Walker Red, he'd become fearless and make bad decisions. When he opened the front gate, the husband came out of the house mad as hell and hit him. Don't forget we were still young, stupid, and in our teens. I never did get those shoes back.

CHAPTER 13

AN AIRBORNE HIPPIE

Sunday morning was my day to go dirt-bike riding. I was out about 6:00 one morning getting ready to ride just as two friends were coming home from partying all night. They were wide awake from whatever they had taken the night before, and they felt like watching me race at Garretson Beach, another place in Brooklyn for riding dirt bikes. The oval track there had a high embankment beyond which was an inlet that went to the beach.

One of my friends was boasting about how he could ride, but he was still drunk and still in his party clothes—a leather jacket and platform shoes. When I came in from racing around the oval track for some water, Vito jumped on the bike and said, "Let me show you how to ride." I had an extra helmet. I said, "Vito, don't kill yourself."

He looked very out of place—a hippie on wheels—but he kick-started the bike and put on the helmet. I don't know what he did next, but the bike took off. Vito just held on tight. He didn't go on the track; he just cut across the center nonstop. That bike was so powerful that he couldn't stop. He rode through the center of the field, where people had pit stops all set up.

Vito shot across the field and kept on going. When he hit the embankment, all you could see was Vito going up into the air and then you didn't see anything—he just disappeared. Everyone was yelling, "Get him off the bike! He's going to kill someone!" We laughed so hard when we got to the top of the embankment and saw Vito sitting on the bike in the middle of the inlet with water in his goggles—we were all dying. We couldn't stop laughing. I wished I had a camera when he came out of the water. His $150 outfit was covered in mud and all kinds of shit. He was expressing some genuine Italian anger. It makes me cry every time I think about such times in my life.

MY TRAVELLING BUDDY

Chapter 14

TWO JOBS AND A TRIP TO ITALY

One time, I got a part-time job at a Dunkin' Donuts across from where I was living. I worked there four hours a day three days a week. The first day was no sweat; I was preparing trays of donuts. And working the counter the second day on the afternoon shift wasn't bad either. However, on the third day, I was asked to do the morning shift at the drive-up window. It started off not so bad, but right after 6:00, the line outside got so long and everything just started to speed up. When I think of that day, I remember watching the *I Love Lucy* episode in which she was working on an assembly line in a candy factory. When the line sped up, she started putting the candy in her month but couldn't keep up.

Sweat was pouring off my face, and I was mixing up orders. That twenty-five minutes felt like forever. The manager took me off that line, and I said goodbye. But later, I told my girlfriend about it, and we laughed for hours. Whenever I see that clip from *I Love Lucy*, it brings tears to my eyes.

I loved working in the bike store building and repairing whatever needed to be fixed. When it was necessary, I'd manufacture any part by transforming scrap metal into a workable part. One day, I was working with Larry on a moped; we debated about the way it was built. The next day at lunch, we came up with a way to modify it and make our own brand of motorbike.

Larry's father, who had been a professional bicycle racer in Italy, still had connections with the Bianchi bike factory. I got a passport and told my mom I was going to Italy. She was at a loss for words; she thought I was kidding, but when she saw the suitcase come out of the closet, she realized I was going.

Larry and I flew to Germany to attend a bike show and see all the new bikes. We walked around with our mouths wide open—unbelievable. We saw some bikes that weren't permitted to come into the United States. They went very fast, and they didn't meet all the local safety laws.

We took a train to Venice. The train was very old; it looked like one you'd see in old war movies. We stayed in a first-class hotel; we had to wear jackets to go to breakfast. Before we got to the dining room, we got shaves complete with hot towels on our faces.

We had to meet up with Mr. Trapltie, a big shot at the bike factory. Larry took care of all the paperwork while I enjoyed the good life. We stayed in Venice for only two nights. The first night, we had dinner in a nice place in a casino. We got around Venice by taxi boats. Our hotel was close, but that night, we missed the last taxi boat, so we tried to walk back. It was 2:00 a.m., and nobody walked around at that time there. Trying to get to the hotel was tough. The only way across the canal was by boat. We had to pay a fisherman a lot of money to take us across.

The last night in the hotel, we used one of the services it offered—we picked up the phone and asked for a lady to be sent up. Larry went first in his room, and then it was my turn in my room. Well, I partied with her. I started to *Waa hoo!* smack her ass and ride her hard. I was making all kinds of wild and loud sounds. I put her in the doggie pose and rode her hard.

Larry came running in after he heard her yelling in Italian, "This guy is crazy!" I had a great time being myself—a wild and crazy guy.

The next day, Larry rented a car and we drove to the bike factory in Milan. We just modified the bikes they had to give them a more American style. We ended up staying there for three weeks. We visited Rome and walked around all day before boarding a plane that left late that night. The Colosseum was unbelievable; it must have been something during Roman times.

When I got home, I had so much to talk about with my parents. Don't forget Italy was where they were from. I was a motor mouth that wouldn't shut up.

EUROPE

ON TO TOKYO

I unpacked and told my parents I was going to Japan. They thought I was just kidding; even after they saw me packing again, they still couldn't believe I was really going.

That was only a week after I had gotten back from Europe. I guess they were happy for me just because I hadn't died in that motorcycle accident. All I knew was that I was back on the road again. My brother and sisters couldn't believe I was really going to Japan for a Kawasaki seminar.

That time, there were three of us. Bobby was to become a new Kawasaki dealer, and Larry already had a dealership in Brooklyn. Everyone on the plane was a Kawasaki dealer going to this seminar. The plane was not very big, but we started to party the second the plane took off. We were drinking, and someone had a joint. I got so wasted. All I remember was that they woke me up and I thought we had landed in Tokyo. When I got off the plane, I was surprised to see a stuffed polar bear on his hind legs in an attack mode. That scared the shit out of me. I found out we were only halfway there. We'd landed in Alaska to refuel.

When we got to Tokyo, guides took us around the city. It was so different from Europe; it was like being at the World's Fair. All the buildings had lights all over them, but the buildings went up only to about sixty-five floors. However, they went down about three or four levels; that was to protect them in case of earthquakes.

Tokyo looked like a mall; I guess that's how the idea of a mall came to be. We took one of those super trains, which was impressive. The young woman who led our tour was a real knockout as you'll see in the pictures at the end of this book. I became real close to Fran. I told her if she came back to the United States with me, I'd marry her.

When she didn't have to work, we went out on our own. She took me to Kyoto, and that was like going back in time seeing the houses and the country.

We parked by this old but well-preserved wooden bridge and walked to a big pond filled with very large goldfish. We went in what I call a little paper house that was an old restaurant. The place looked so delicate even though it has been there for a long time. On the small tables were wood-burning woks; we sat on the floor. I was the life of the party; it was the first time they'd seen someone who used chopsticks with two hands.

Back in Tokyo one night, Larry, Bobby, Steve, a couple of other dealers, and I went out for a night on the town not far from our hotel, the Pacific Hotel, a five-star place that had knives and forks as well as chairs around the tables.

Tokyo was very exciting—a lot of people were going up and down steps that looked just like stairs leading down to subway stations but didn't. All buildings in Tokyo had two and sometimes three levels down—another city but with casinos. It looked like a hole in the wall, and we felt we were walking into a cave. We went to a disco; in its center was a round dance floor that would go around and also up and then down to the floor below just like a giant glass elevator. Some people were dancing while other were just along for the ride. When we left, we were feeling kind of toasted.

Trying to cross the street was another thrilling adventure—the traffic traveled in the opposite direction, and it was tough to cross five lanes. We hailed a small cab and tried to tell the driver where we wanted to go. It seemed we were there for an hour and a half; our driver got so crazy, but we didn't know what he was saying. He got out red-faced and was yelling at us. Then we found out it was against the law to squeeze that many people into one cab.

We were in Tokyo for almost three weeks. Kawasaki was a lot bigger manufacturer than I had imagined. The company made everything, even ocean liners. The Kawasaki plant seemed to be on its own island; it took us more than a week to see the whole plant. When I got home, I had so much to show and tell everybody.

The next month, the bike shop received the first shipment of mopeds and minibikes from Italy. Larry got a van, and we loaded up one of each model—a moped, a folding motorbike, and a mini dirt bike along with some brochures. We went to dealers in Long Island to see if they would sell the line of bikes we had created.

Making the brochure was also a lot of fun. I rode the mini dirt bike on the track in Garrison Beach, and Larry's father took pictures for our brochure. That is the only item I had a hard time finding; I wanted to show it in the back of the book with my photos.

I love to show off the pictures I took on my travel adventures especially to girls. I used to take girls into my room and show a lot more than my pictures. We lived in a big house, and my bedroom was next to my sister's room. One day, I showed my pictures to my sister's girlfriend. She'd always sleep over on Saturday, and when everyone was asleep, I used to get her out of my sister's room and into mine. I guess that was why she enjoyed spending the night at my house.

Larry's father did something no one was ready for; he went to the store one morning and didn't come home. He flew to Italy, where he set up a whole different life in a big villa with a beautiful woman. He left everything and didn't look back.

One thing he left was a thirty-two-foot, twin-screw Owens, a wooden cabin cruiser. It held six people, and it was moored at the Mill Basin Yacht Club in Brooklyn. I used to go all the time and keep it clean for him, so he gave me a key for the electric gate at the yacht club. I was always taking girls to my boat, as I called it. I never took it out; the girls would see a lot of the cabin.

JAPAN

JAPAN

THE STOVE STORY, THE GARAGE DOOR STORY, AND LORRAINE

I always think about all the bad things I did that drove my parents wild. One night after partying till 5:00 a.m., I found myself sitting in the kitchen thinking of something to do for my mother. I decided to clean the stove. I thought it would be a nice surprise for her to come down and find a clean stove.

When they came down Sunday morning at about 8:00, my parents were so surprised. There was fire in my father's eyes; he was cursing me in Italian and wanted to kill me. You see, I'd taken the stove completely apart. Parts were all over the kitchen. I couldn't put it back together, so they had to go to Sears that day for a new one.

Another time, I had taken my father's car, which was parked in front of the house. When I got home, I thought it would be nice to put the car in the garage. I backed the car down the driveway. I had to stop to open the garage door, so I threw it in park and got out. The car took off and drove through the garage door. I'd put the car in reverse instead of park. At 5:00 a.m., the sound of the car going throw the garage door could be heard from blocks away. So could my father's yelling when he came out.

They were real happy when I settled down. It was the time Son of Sam was on the loose killing whomever he felt like killing. Everyone was afraid to go out to clubs. He mainly followed couples from clubs to their cars. We were out in Brooklyn in a club called Beef Steak Charlie's where they had the *Gong Show*. People would go onstage and do something. If they were bad, they were gonged and had to get off the stage. Son of Sam was there that night and followed the last couple he shot. They went down to Shore Parkway and parked to make out. They were his last victims.

I took home a girl named Lorraine I had met that night, and we talked for hours. She told me she didn't want to go home, so I told her to come home with me. We lived in a bedroom of my mothers' house for about four years, and then we moved into my attic apartment I had mentioned; we were happy.

Two years later, we wanted to start a family, so we got married and had a great wedding. We took an Amtrak train to Disneyland; we had one of those little rooms with a fold-down bunk bed. I had gotten something that would be fun—some underwear with four leg holes; that meant we could both wear them at the same time. Can you imagine us trying to get up into the bunk bed?

Disneyland was hot. Instead of walking around the park, I rented a helicopter to fly us around Disney. When we hit an air pocket, the helicopter dropped about fifteen feet, and Larraine was holding on for dear life as you'll see in a photo I took just as we hit the air pocket. When we got home, I took her on a cruise, and we had a great time.

MY WEDDING AFTER

ONE WEEK

CHAPTER 17

WE'RE A FAMILY

A year later, Frankie was born. When I saw him being born, I told Lorraine I was going to stay home and be Mr. Mom. I started showing him numbered flash cards when he was three days old, and I didn't stop. He became a walking calculator.

We then had Jeannine. I went a different route with her; I got her into reading, and now she's studying to become a pharmacist.

I told you life doesn't stop changing. Sometimes when people want to change, they pay a price that can really hurt. They can feel like lost children, and the feeling can stay with them for the rest of their lives.

I ran into an old Brooklyn friend; I'd gone to school with his kid sister, and when he told me where she lived, I was shocked—she lived just minutes away. She and I got together and talked about old times and the changes we were going through. She talked about Virginia Beach and said she wanted to move there. She knew people there who would help her put her life back together.

We went down to Midland Beach in Staten Island to hang out and talk. We parked in the lot. Just as the windows were starting to fog up, we heard a loud tapping on the window. It was a cop. We'd been busted. We got out of the car, and we couldn't stop laughing. The cop asked us what was so funny, but all I could say was, "Sorry, officer." That put a smile on her face. It wasn't as if we were kids anymore, but I couldn't stop laughing. The officer gave us both $50 tickets. We laughed every time we brought the story up. She's that friend I have in Virginia Beach. I like it there. I miss the house I had on the beach.

Like I said, life don't stop; it just changes. Look at me now—I'm overweight, always in pain, and have no more money. But I'll never stop laughing. There's so much more I could write about, but I'll just say goodbye.

Life Just Doesn't Stop
It Only Gets Better

My best friend Diana Urgo

ABOUT THE BOOK

I was one of those kids who were always getting hurt—you know, the one who was always trying to outdo the other guy. Even when I didn't try, I got hurt. One day, I was on my dirt bike in Garretson Beach. The day was a hot eighty-seven degrees with clear skies. After riding about three hours, I stopped to get a drink. I put the kickstand down, and while I was walking to my car—*bang!* I fell down, got up, and started seeing double. People were running over to help me. They were flying remote-controlled airplanes by the beach, and someone had lost control of a plane. It had crash-landed hard on the back of the head. It was a good thing I hadn't taken my helmet off; I would have been seriously hurt otherwise, but I sustained an injury to my neck that I can still feel thirty-five years later.

That's just one of my misadventures. Read about more in this book.